Innocent AGAIN

3 Keys to Joy Restored
After Childhood Sexual Abuse

By Jeanette Finn

www.InnocentAgain.com

Published with help from 100X Publishing, Olympia, WA

ISBN: 979-8-9850307-0-9

Printed in the United States of America

For those who desire to be

Innocent Again

Table of Contents

Introduction

This book is for the one in four girls who have been sexually abused before they turned 18 years old and realize that now, as adults, the impact of that trespass has taken away their joy. They have relationship struggles. They don't know how to set boundaries. They are scared to be intimate. They have a difficult time trusting. They have trouble with work, making it difficult to get or keep a job. They have issues with self-medicating. They use food, alcohol, drugs, sex, gambling, shopping...any means they can to keep their shame at bay. Sadly, many of them don't even recognize how this destructive behavior is driven by the suppressed emotions and secrets of childhood sexual abuse.

I am going to approach this subject from this angle: You have been contemplating the issues in your life that you are not happy with, the things causing you pain, the things that aren't working. Maybe it's health, wealth, addictions, depression, or relationship issues because of not acknowledging and releasing the impact that sexual abuse had on you. You are beginning to question the connection between the abuse and your lack of a joy-filled life.

There are three different camps you could be in. Camp one: You are just now starting to entertain the idea that what happened to you did affect you and continuing to deny it isn't working. You are unable to stop your destructive behaviors of self-medicating, and it is destroying your life. **You want help to heal now.**

Camp two: You know what happened to you affected you, and you have been trying to overcompensate for it. You've been very successful on the outside. Everything appears good, but you are falling apart on the inside. You feel like you are about to implode. **You want help to heal now.**

Camp three: Your life is falling apart right at this moment, it has already fallen apart or a major life event has caused you to take a long, hard look at where you are at. You are tired of the secret and how it has kept you powerless. You are ready to work through the process. **You want help to heal now.**

Of course, all three of these camps are in Victim Village. None of us survivors of sexual abuse were responsible for our abuse, which makes us victims, but there is no power in staying a victim. Victim Village can be a very comfortable place for a while, but when you stay there too long, you lose your power. Believe me, I know. I stayed there a long time. I would start moving out, and then get scared of the unknown and move right back in. It's like I started living on the outskirts of Victim Village, getting close to freedom, but remained a victim. It took a life event for me to finally get fully moved out and get my power back.

You do have power, even though as a child (or even as an adult) it was taken from you. You can take it back. It is yours for the taking, but you do have to do the taking. There are doors you need to walk through. You are no longer going to live as a victim; it's time to live as a victor!

In this book, I will share good news: Victims of sexual abuse can be set free from shame and guilt and be *Innocent Again*! In this journey of healing, we will be going through three doors that lead to three connected rooms. Each door needs a key, and I will be giving you the keys my Heavenly Daddy gave me to open those doors. When you do, you, too, can be *Innocent Again* and have full, overflowing joy. This healing process will take you back and forth between these rooms, renewing your mind, reclaiming your identity, and restoring your joy. You can read the book through and learn about each room, and then go back to the room you feel would help you most in your healing process, or you can enter the first room and stay there awhile to get familiar with it.

Everyone's healing process is different. As you heal, you will be revisiting the rooms. This is not a one and done event. There will be renewing, reclaiming, and restoring throughout your journey here on earth. I am humbled and honored to be on the journey with you and to share the three keys to help you!

Before we start opening doors, let's look at where we are starting.

Chapter 1

You Are Not Alone

In the introduction, I mentioned a statistic: 25% of girls get sexually abused before the age of 18. When I consider the hundreds of women I have met on my journey to *Innocent Again*, I believe it's more like double that number. Also, being sexually abused by someone you know, which happens 93% of the time when abused as a child, makes it even more difficult to report. The shame, guilt, and confusion are terrifying. And that is one more reason the number is most likely higher. Besides that, the way our western culture sexualizes women, I would dare to say that 98% of women are sexually abused by media. What we see from movies and media about what it means to be a woman causes us to question our their worth beyond our bodies.

Whatever was done to you is unique to you, because no two situations of sexual abuse are the same. Even siblings abused by the same person in the same household is not the same. Why? Because our personality types process the abuse differently. However, the impact on our femininity is the same and the process of our healing is the same. But your abuse, just because it is different than someone else's, does not make you alone. With baking, the same sugar goes into making a cake, a cookie, or a doughnut, yet all these things turn out differently. The same is true of your sweetness. We are all sweet inside and look different on the outside. Our sweetness got taken away in a variety of ways, and we are not alone. It is not what happened to you, but the effect it had on your femininity and sexuality that matters. If you are not comfortable in your own skin, this book is for you.

In this format, when I don't have any way to guard who reads this book, I will not go into details of abuse. I do not want to trigger a reader who does not have the emotional support they need. I do not want to risk arousing an offender who may have picked it up for just that reason. I will not give examples of what may appear to be minor and major abuse. It is more about how you feel about being a woman that plays into sexual abuse, how empowered or disempowered you feel as a woman, how you value womanhood. Some of the smallest things can deeply, negatively impact your sense of sexuality and femininity.

Again, I want to say you are not alone in having been sexually abused, no matter the level of abuse it was. Even if it didn't involve anything physical, you can be sexually abused emotionally. This is why I believe nearly 100% of women are abused in the western culture because of media, and even sadder are the women who are duped and participate in making it so.

There are an estimated 39 million adult survivors who live in America today. ***You are not alone.***

Questions to contemplate as you restore your joy:

~ ~ ~ ~ ~

Do you feel less alone now?

Do you recognize that sexual abuse doesn't have to be physical?

Have you ever considered media to be sexually abusive?

~ ~ ~ ~ ~

Chapter 2

You Are Loved

Hopefully you now realize the enormity of sexual abuse and that you are not alone. Now, I want to talk to you about being loved. You have a Heavenly Father. You are not an accident. This world we live in was not an accident. There was not some big bang that somehow created every living thing, plant, animal, human...

No, there is a unique design to all of it and all of us. There is a master Architect who designed this amazing world we live in. Did you know there are over 17,500 species of butterflies? How anyone could think that this whole creation happened by accident takes more faith than believing in a Divine Creator. I am not here to convince you. I am here to help you on your journey to *Innocent Again*, and that journey begins with knowing there is more than this physical life here on earth. We are spiritual beings having a physical experience. Our whole earthly experience is for us to grow spiritually. It is by being stuck in these earth suits that we grow our spiritual selves. We are here on earth to grow spiritually. This time here on earth is temporary. We are all going to leave this physical dimension one day, and while we are here, we can grow spiritually.

I don't know what part of the journey you are on with God or if you are even on a journey with Him yet. You may be asking, "If God loved me, why would He have let that bad happen to me? You may not have wanted to consider having a relationship with a God who would let that happen to you. But here's the deal as I understand it. Keep in mind I am no theologian. I have, however, almost three decades of walking with the Lord, and that isn't to say my walk has all been perfect. Far from it, but that's the point. The point is growth. The point is learning. The point is having a relationship with the Creator of the universe. That is the way He designed it.

Can you even imagine that the Creator of the universe wants a personal relationship with you? He designed you with a God-shaped hole only He can fill. As we walk with our Daddy, we begin to know Him and understand some of His ways. He will always remain a mystery, and part of this journey in life is trying to discover those mysteries.

He hasn't hidden things from you; He has hidden

things *for* you.

Since you are reading this book and you picked it up for healing from sexual abuse, you are looking for information to help you in your healing. I know God is part of that help. You don't need to make a decision now whether you believe or don't believe. All I want you to do right now, if you don't already believe in God, is to consider it. Consider that there is a Heavenly Creator, and He has a plan and purpose for you.

He has hidden things <u>for</u> you.

He loves you! ***You are loved!***

Questions to contemplate as you restore your joy:

~ ~ ~ ~ ~

Do you believe in God? If not, are you willing to consider it?

What was your family's beliefs about God?

Do you have a difficult time thinking about God as a loving Father?

~ ~ ~ ~ ~

Chapter 3

Start Where You Are

What does your life look like right now? What are your relationships like? How is your job going? How is your health? What are your thought processes saying? What is your environment like? Is your house clean? Are there dirty dishes in the sink? Is your bed made? Is there a pile of laundry that needs to be cleaned or a clean pile of laundry that needs to be put away? Or both?

With the title of this chapter, I want us to invite God into our current situation, no matter what a mess it may be. The whole thing about having a relationship with God is that He loves you just as you are. As a matter of fact, there's nothing you can do to make Him love you more and there's nothing you can do to make Him love you less. He *is* love, and love is what He does. He knew every choice you were going to make before you ever made them, and He loves you anyway. He loves you even if you don't believe He exists. He wants to have a relationship with you.

Getting Joy Restored in my life started with inviting

God into my mess. Personally, I was mad at Him. I felt like He had let me down. My marriage of 20 years ended in a horrible divorce. I was drinking, smoking, jobless, and in the middle of a great big pity party. It was right in that mess when I invited Him in. I told Him, "If You knew everything about me, You knew I would end up here, so here I am." I believe if I hadn't done that step, I would still be in that mess and not sober, drug free, and happily remarried with a career I love.

A lot of people believe they need to get their lives more cleaned up before they start trying to have a relationship with God. That's just not true. He already knows where you are at. He already knows how you are trying to numb the pain. He already knows the ways you are trying to escape. He is waiting for you to invite Him in. He's a gentleman; He will knock patiently. He will not push Himself on you.

I would talk to God while I was drunk and stoned. I started believing He could help me out of my situation, and that I didn't need to get out of the situation before He would help me. He wanted to help me. I started believing He *could* help me. Trying and failing, I knew I couldn't get myself out of that situation. God and I together got me out of that situation! All I am asking of you, my friend, is to open your mind enough to what may be a new thought for you: Believe He can help you *in* the mess, and you do not need to clean up the mess first.

One perspective that helped me in this process was to see God as my invisible friend. I would visualize Him sitting next to me. He would be the passenger in the car. Jesus would be driving down the road with me. I would talk to Him like He was there, because you know what? He is.

I had learned of Jesus years earlier and even done the salvation prayer, but I had never really considered He was there for me in my daily life. That is, until my life got so bad, I was willing to start having a personal relationship with Him. I started learning for myself through varies books, teachings, seminars, and Bible studies about God, Jesus, and the Holy Spirit. I am excited to share with you some of what I have learned. My hope is that it will help you to want to have a personal relationship with Jesus and become *Innocent Again*.

Don't concern yourself right now with what you think you know about God, what you think you need to change in your life, or what you think He will want you to change in your life first. Just invite Him into your life as it is. Leave your preconceived ideas behind. This is all about having a personal relationship with Him. He is going to fill that God space inside of you so you can have Joy Restored. You can be *Innocent Again*.

Get ready for the next several chapters where we will talk about the three keys to Joy Restored. I look forward to sharing them with you! ***Start where you are!***

Questions to contemplate as you restore your joy:

~ ~ ~ ~ ~

Do you feel like you are supposed to clean up your mess before you can invite God in?

Do you blame God for what happened to you?

Do you think you know what God wants from you, so you don't want to have a relationship with Him?

~ ~ ~ ~ ~

First Key:

Renew Your Mind

Chapter 4

You Are Not Your Thoughts

What are you thinking about?

That reminds me of a cute joke, especially since I do have German heritage. An English boat was taking on water off the German coast. The captain contacts the German coast guard and says, "Mayday, mayday, this is the UK39 and we are sinking. I repeat, we are sinking." A couple moments pass by with no answer. The captain repeats, "Mayday, mayday, this is the UK39 and we are sinking. I repeat, we are sinking." This time the German coast guard replies, "Vot are you sinking about?" Ha!

Have you ever thought about your thinking? Do you realize you can choose your thoughts? You don't have to think about or dwell on whatever pops into your head. As a matter of fact, what is naturally popping into your head is probably something unhelpful, anxious, or negative; something you don't want to think about. Maybe even your thinking right now isn't the best. There is an amazing truth though: You can pick thoughts to think on purpose.

You can and will think thoughts that are good for you after you have read this book and developed your personal relationship with God. He designed you and He designed your mind. He has given you the ability to renew your mind. He knew from the beginning that renewing your mind would be a key to living a life of joy. I am sure you've heard it said, and if it not, here it is for you for the first time: It's not what happens to you that matters most, but how you think about what happened to you that matters most.

This is such a profound thing. Your thoughts determine your future. It is not to downplay what has happened to you, especially since this book is about overcoming a horrible thing, sexual abuse. Sexual abuse so profoundly messes with the mind, body, and soul. How could you possibly see something that was bad as good? Isn't that what I am asking you to do? No, certainly not. I am not asking you to do that at all. You cannot think away your abuse, but I am trying to help you with your thinking. Becoming aware that you can choose what you are thinking about is an important turning point.

If you are so busy thinking how what happened to

you was bad, unfair, and ruined your life, then that is where you will stay. I'm also not saying that isn't true. What happened to you *was* bad, unfair, and ruined you in some ways, but you don't have to stay a victim. You can be a victor. If you want your offender to still have that kind of power over you, continuing to harm you over and over in your imagination, then don't change your thinking. Thinking about what you don't want or how bad things were only brings more of it. Complaining brings what you are complaining about.

Here's what I am asking: Think about believing you can be healed. You can have a joy filled life even though you were a victim. The key word in that last sentence is...*were*. You do not need to stay a victim.

Thoughts have energy. You want to start becoming aware of the energy you are creating. Is a certain thought helpful or hurtful to you? The energy of a thought is like a seed that will grow in your life. What kind of seeds are you planting? You weren't in control of what happened to you, but you are in control of your thoughts now. Thoughts are the seeds to action. You respond to your thoughts. You act because of your thoughts. Your thoughts create emotions. You act on those emotions. You need to become aware of what you are thinking about. That is the first step in renewing your mind.

What are you thinking?

Your thoughts themselves are not real. But the fact that you can think is real. Now, it's up to you to think the thoughts that will help you heal. Anyone who has the Holy Spirit living in them has the power to do this. Because you have a Heavenly Father who wants the best for you, He made a way for you to have an abundant life. He gave you the ability to choose. Choose Him. Choose healing thoughts. Renew your mind.

Here's something to ponder: If your thoughts aren't real, but they create, and you can choose what to think, thereby choosing what to create, then why not choose thoughts that will give you the best future?

> ***Thoughts are not reality.***

You are not your thoughts. You are a spiritual being in a human body having a thought. You are the observer of the thought. Those thoughts make you feel and have emotions, which you become aware of. Do you want to change the way you feel? Then change the way you think. You can change the thought.

Thoughts are not reality. Reality is what is happening right now outside of your mind. Your thoughts are either in the future or in the past, unless you deliberately put them in the now. After reading this book, I hope you are able to do more deliberate thinking and be in the moment, because that is where the joy is. The past is not real. The future is not real. Worry and anxiety are imaginary thoughts. So, if you want to change your reality, change your thoughts. And we must first begin with becoming aware of our thoughts.

For example, I use to sell a product that helped utilize more space in kitchen cabinets and drawers. I would go to my client's home and design a plan. They could then purchase the product and have it installed. One particular client wanted to think about it. As I left and was driving home, I started thinking about the fact that when they want to think about it, they usually don't buy. The thought of wasting my time driving out there (one hour each way) came up. I started imagining the next morning's call – her telling me she had decided to not make the improvement for her kitchen. I started feeling icky, but then became aware of not liking how I was feeling. Pausing, I considered my thinking. I felt God say to me, "You don't know which way this is going to go. For now, why don't you imagine calling in the morning and her saying, 'Yes, I would love to move forward with the whole project, including all the extra options you gave us.'"

Instantly I started grinning ear to ear. The whole atmosphere in my car changed. I was like, "Yes! I got the sale. I feel so good. I can imagine that I got the sale all night long and tomorrow morning and feel good about it. I don't have to imagine the worst."

You know what, I can't even remember now if I got that sale or not. All I remember is going from being upset to happy in a moment just by changing my thinking about something. I didn't have any control of it in the moment, but I did have control of what I could think about it.

Another aspect to consider about your thinking is that it is a learned behavior. You think the way you think because of how you were raised. Everything about this human experience is learned. Nothing happened to you instantly, even physical growth was a slow process. Learning to walk and talk...all slow processes and neither just happened. The only thing that just happens is your physical body's changes, little by little, without you having to do anything. The aging process is the only thing that *just happens*. Time is going to pass, and your body will change. You can do things to help the process go smoother, and we will talk about that in a later chapter, but for now, recognize that you think the way you think because of what you learned by association, observing the people around you, and your experiences.

What you think about money, what you think about relationships, what you think about government…it is all from what you learned as a child. If you haven't taken the time to question why it is you think the way you do, you are still just a product of your upbringing.

Only you can change the way you think. Only you can learn and get new information to decide what you believe. You don't know what you don't know until you search and learn and get more information in order to make your own decision.

Questions to contemplate as you restore your joy:

~ ~ ~ ~ ~

Has this chapter got you thinking about your thinking?

Have you ever realized you had this much control of your thinking?

Are you going to take the time to become an observer of your thoughts?

~ ~ ~ ~ ~

Chapter 5

Seeing Differently

Now that you've learned some interesting things about your thoughts, let's delve a little deeper. Your brain is a physical organ. You can't control it, just like you can't control your heart. Your heart is going to beat automatically. Your brain is going to have thoughts. It constantly processes what happens around it, taking in information from all five senses. It has been doing this from birth, and in this process has formed automatic thoughts and automatic responses to those thoughts. What you now need to learn is how you have the power to override those automatic thoughts and responses.

For example, let's say as a child you were bit by a German Shepherd. One day, as an adult, you are on a leisurely stroll with a friend, and further down the path you notice a German Shepherd. Your brain instantly gives you a thought and a response to *run away as fast as you can*. You override that thought with another thought (not wanting to look like a scaredy cat to your friend), so you are able to choose a different response and don't run away. Basically, you have chosen to see how the automatic thought and response were not the right ones in this current situation. That is the power of using your mind over your brain. Your mind is more powerful than your brain.

You do have the ability to choose what you think, and therefore chose your response. That doesn't mean it will be easy. Thoughts are going to pop into your head, but you get to decide what to do with them. That's what seeing differently is all about – taking the time to recognize what you are thinking about.

When sexual abuse has occurred as a child, guaranteed there will be distorted thinking on many levels. Issues with authority, trust, protection, sexuality, relationships, self-worth to name a few. Want a practical strategy to align your thought life with biblical truth to help you live a joy-filled life? Let me help you renew your mind.

In order to see things differently and think differently, you get to take the time to step back and observe yourself. You were created to be able to do that. Just like the German Shepherd example, before taking off running, you choose to look at the situation outside of yourself, to predict the future. You were able to make a choice to choose the response, the action you wanted to take that would better suit you. You were able to choose a future result you wanted: to not look like a scaredy cat in front of your friend.

You are responsible for what you choose to think and dwell on. I am not trying to say this is an easy process...thinking about what you are thinking about takes effort. Most people never take the time or make the effort. They just let the thoughts flow in and out and react and remain in the habits and lifestyles they are accustomed to. Basically, the brain is lazy and doesn't want to take the effort to think new things, which is how and why habits are created. Ninety-five percent of what you do is from habit. All habits are brain based. You can change your habits and create new ones; habits that will give you the joy you want in life.

You are not a victim. You can control your thoughts and responses. You do have a choice. You can choose to see things differently. You are a multifaceted human being created in God's image which allows you to see things from many different angles or perspectives. The way you choose to perceive things becomes a way of thinking, a habit, a mindset.

Your mindset is a collection of thoughts and beliefs. Your mindset determines how you handle situations – the way you sort out what is going on and what you should do. It shapes how you see and interact with the world. Here's the interesting thing about your mindset. Before you were even able to choose, your mindset was formed. See, your brain has been being shaped by your environment. It is like a computer, gathering information and processing it from birth. If you are interested in learning more about the development of your brain, there is plenty of scientific information available. But for purposes of this book, I am not going to go there. For now, it is enough for you to know that you didn't have a choice as a child as to what your mindset was going to be like; it was purely shaped by your environment. But there is good news! As an adult, now you can choose your mindset. If you don't like the way things are going in your life, you can change the way you see things and things will change.

Every moment of every day, your brain and body are physically reacting and responding to the thoughts running through your mind. Your mindset determines the tone your thoughts have on you; a tone of victim or victor. Understanding how mindsets form and how they change your thinking helps you understand the power of your thoughts and how to change your mind to think thoughts of victor, not victim. The correct tone (mindset) is crucial to restoring joy in your life. The ability to think, feel, choose and build thoughts into mindsets is one of the most powerful things God has given us!

Essentially, the way you think, through mindsets you adopt, influences your words and actions. In turn, these words and actions determine your emotional healing from childhood sexual abuse and the level of joy you will have in your life. You can make the choice to change a victim mindset to a victor mindset. You get to choose what you want to believe. You get to control your thinking. You get to develop a mindset that serves you. You get to create a life of joy! You are a victor not a victim.

You will need to take the time to figure out your current mindset, because you were a victim when you got abused. Your thinking isn't going to change that. You were abused, and sometimes to figure out your mindset, you will need to talk about what happened to you with a safe person or in a safe group. You will need to shine light into the darkness. What's kept in the dark can't heal. Your journey to healing will be unique to you. I am not saying you will have to pour through every traumatic thing that happened to you, but you will need to give a voice to what happened so you can become aware of the mindset and thinking that got created because of the abuse. The abuse affected the way you see the world...and not in a good way.

Abuse affected the way you see the world.

You are now going to look at the ways you think and the mindsets you have so you can align yourself with our Heavenly Father instead; He has a good plan for you.

Questions to contemplate as you restore your joy:

~ ~ ~ ~ ~

Have you ever considered what kind of mindsets you have?

What mindsets were put on you about God when you were a child?

What mindsets were put on you about your value?

~ ~ ~ ~ ~

Chapter 6

No More Fear

As you begin to become aware of your thoughts and mindsets you will be able to change them. God has given us this ability. He wouldn't have asked us to do it if He hadn't given us the ability. In His word He says to renew your mind. As you begin to understand and realize how much power you have in your mind, you will start using your thoughts to work for you instead of against you.

We were designed to have a joy mindset, which doesn't mean things will always be easy, but it does mean we can shift our focus. We can renew our minds. In the scientific world it is called neuro-plasticity, and it is the ability God gave us to be able to transform into His image. It's how babies and young children learn; they observe, mimic, and copy what they see others doing. It's also how all of us form new neuron pathways and connections in our brains as we learn new things and grow in understanding. Jesus said we could have His joy and our joy could be made full. That's what this journey on earth, in these physical bodies, in this time dimension, is all about: being transformed into His image. This is a place for us to grow, learn, and overcome.

When we are young, it's happening naturally. We grow and learn many different things as we develop, such as learning to eat on our own, how to walk and talk, potty training, and more. This growth process happens automatically, and we can't even stop it. We will grow, and we are going to go from crawling to walking, needing to be fed to feeding ourselves, from having diapers changed to using the toilet.

During this physical growth and learning, because our bodies are changing, our brain is growing and learning as well, automatically taking things in and storing information for future use. Our brain is the reason we can learn to walk, talk, and feed ourselves. It sends the messages to our bodies to make the moves to accomplish these things. As we move past being a toddler and enter the school system, it forces us to learn with a new focus: mental learning, such as reading, writing, and arithmetic. In the US, this process of education goes on for 12 years, until around age 18. That's when most people stop learning. They stop trying to gain more knowledge, and by doing that, stay very limited in their life experiences, especially for those of us who have been sexually abused.

Survivors of Childhood Sexual Abuse (CSA) have a lot of unlearning to do, and that can only be done by gaining new knowledge intentionally. It won't happen automatically. It won't happen by force. It's not required by law. You get to choose it. You get to take the time to get the truth about who you really are and who God made you to be. The fact that you are reading this means you have made that choice. You are on this journey of healing and having joy restored to the full, to being *Innocent Again*. God send His only Son Jesus so that you could have abundant life. I am so proud of you! If we were face to face right now, I would give you a big hug!

This may not be the easiest learning you have ever done. It might even be the hardest thing you have ever done, because this learning isn't only about taking information in and applying it. You are examining what kind of information you currently use to process the world around you. It can be challenging. You will have to unlearn.

God helped me understand this for myself by giving me an analogy. He knows what helps me to learn just like He knows what will help you to learn. He said to me (not in audible words, but through my thoughts and imagination, kind of like a download, a concept that I could instantly grasp):

"It's like wearing a pair of sunglasses that you were given as a child. You didn't have a choice as to what sunglasses were put on you, and the way you saw the world was impacted by those sunglasses. I am so pleased that you have come to recognize they are not the sunglasses I designed for you to wear. They have given you a distorted view of the world, not the view I designed for it. We are now on a journey together to help you remove those sunglasses. It won't be instant, because there are several shades and hues to the world I created. I designed this world to be a process, a place for growth. All growth takes time. Look at the caterpillar turning into a butterfly, look at the apple seed turning into an apple, consider even how you came into this world – a little seed that grew in your mother's womb. So, also, when it comes to growing into your true identity in Me, it will take time. The sunglasses you are wearing are not the ones I have designed for you, but they are a great place to start. In our walk together in this journey to *Innocent Again,* you will be putting on different sunglasses as we progress

> ***This is a journey toward joy and in joy.***

through it. Your change, like the butterflies, will go through different processes. You will see things differently in each process just like changing sunglasses changes your view of the scenery around you. What I really want you to take account of right now is that My love, peace, and joy are complete in you this very moment. This is a journey towards joy and in joy. Your joy can start right now. Your joy is not about the circumstances, not about the sunglasses you are wearing. Your joy is complete right now, in this moment, and as we are together, I will help you discover this."

Let's break down this analogy a bit more. Remember how I mentioned that it may be the hardest learning you've ever done since it involves unlearning? The reason it can be so hard is because unlearning requires you to realize what you have learned. It can be very scary, especially as a survivor of CSA, to take off those glasses and really look at them. Most of us have been pretending that what happened didn't impact us, and by not thinking about it and pushing it away, we think we're all good. Since you have this book in your hands or eBook on your device and are reading these words, I suspect you have come to realize that hasn't worked for you. I am so proud of you for being brave enough to take the time to heal. You deserve to live a life of joy and to not be encumbered by the past.

The good news is that you do not have to take this journey alone and you don't need to be afraid. God has not given you a spirit of fear, but of power, and of love, and of a sound mind. You will be supported all along the way. *Innocent Again* will be there for you with the tools to help you have a life of joy in Christ.

Let's get a new pair of sunglasses!

Questions to contemplate as you restore your joy:

~ ~ ~ ~ ~

When was the last time you learned something new?

What has been guiding your decisions in life? What pair of sunglasses have you been wearing?

~ ~ ~ ~ ~

Second Key:

Reclaim Your Identity

Chapter 7

There is Nothing Wrong with You

Wrong things, bad things, unforgettable things happened to you, but that does not mean anything is wrong with you. It did impact the way you viewed the world around you though. It did impact the choices you made. It did impact your thinking, which is paramount to the level of joy you are experiencing in your life. You may have made wrong choices because of the sexual abuse you experienced; I know I did (feel free to read about some of them in my first book called *Girl Distorted*), but that does not make us wrong or bad. It makes us human. All of us make bad decisions, but as a survivor of CSA, you have a level of shame you took on as a child that makes you feel like you are bad. Shame says, "Something is wrong with you, and you somehow did something to cause the abuse." Shame lies and is never an appropriate feeling regarding being a survivor of CSA.

For survivors of childhood sexual abuse, shame is a pervasive feeling that grows and thrives as years go by until it is addressed. It slows healing, prevents self-acceptance, and can lead a person to all kinds of avoidance techniques in attempts to combat the sexual abuse trauma or cover it up. Shame and guilt get tangled up for survivors of CSA. We are going to do some untangling of that now.

Guilt is an emotion that does have a positive side at times; it can stop us from continuing to do things we know we shouldn't. Anger has a positive side too, but both these emotions get more attention for their negative side. We have all seen people who can't control their anger, have a disposition for anger, or are easily enraged, which is an unhealthy emotion. That is the negative side of anger. As survivors of CSA, we tend to go to the negative side of guilt moving towards shame, an unhealthy emotion that has no value. Shame says *you are bad*, guilt says *you did a bad thing*. Shame is useless, because *you* are never bad. You may have done a bad thing and feel guilty about it, but you, yourself, your personhood is not bad. You are a child of the King. You are royalty! My job is to help you to know that.

When you feel guilty, you can to a self-check and see what it was you did that made you feel that way. Did you snap at your friend, your spouse, your kids? Did you talk negatively about someone behind their back? Did you eat the whole bag of chips? Feeling guilty or bad about these things is your conscience, or I like to say the Holy Spirit is giving you a nudge that you could have made a better choice. Guilt is not to condemn you, but it helps you be aware of changes you can make in your behavior so you can have the results you want. Repentance is always an appropriate response to guilt. Repentance is a turning away from what you did wrong, making a different, better choice, and then releasing the feeling of guilt.

Shame, on the other hand, is when your whole self feels wrong. Shame whispers, "If they only knew, they would want nothing to do with you." Shame from childhood sexual abuse separates us from others even though that is the very thing we were made for: relationships. Relationship with God, others, and ourselves. You think something is wrong with you, but just like the title of this chapter says...*there is nothing wrong with you.*

As human beings, we constantly try to put things in a box, label it, and be on to the next thing. When something similar comes up again, then we know what box to put it in. Even as kids we want to do this because that is how our brains work, but from our limited experiences, we usually don't put the item in the right box. Sometimes we are so young that we don't even have a box to choose yet. We don't even know that box (or any box) exists. As young people, much of the time we don't even have the words to process the feelings going on inside of us. As adult survivors, we need to give a voice to what happened so we can get those emotions and feelings into the right box that will bring healing and joy into our lives.

Now is the time to reclaim your true identity. Now is the time to open the boxes and get rid of the lies about who you are. To get rid of those lies, they must be acknowledged first, or else they cannot be learned from, grown from, or processed. To break free from being stuck in a lie, you must first identify the lies you believe. You are exposing your wounds to the light. You can't heal something if you haven't named it. Healing an emotional wound is like healing a physical wound; there are steps, processes, and then time. You can't get to the next step until you acknowledge the step you are on.

Acknowledging that you feel like something is wrong with you brings awareness, and awareness brings choices. Like you've already learned, you can choose a better way to think. You can put on a new pair of sunglasses.

Healing is available for you. You are on the path of becoming who our Daddy always meant you to be.

You are going to start doing things differently. You are going to become an observer of your life, thoughts, and actions. The traumatic experiences of your life won't destroy you. They will make you stronger. Healing is a mindset – a spiritual process whereby you leave behind an old way of being, and fundamentally embrace a new relationship to life.

God will restore what has been taken from you. That is what He has made available to you through His Son Jesus. Jesus Christ is the way to God. When you believe Jesus died for your sins and rose from the grave, you have a new identity in Christ. You have direct access to God in prayer. You have been made new. You now have the Holy Spirt living in you. The Holy Spirit gives you the power to make the changes in your life and thinking about that will bring you joy! If this is new information to you, I would love to tell you more. Please reach out to me at support@InnocentAgain.com. I also recommend reading the Gospel of John in the Bible.

> ***Healing is available for you.***

From this point forward, choose to believe God loves you, and knowing He loves you opens the door to healing. It is on this beautiful journey of healing where you will begin to understand some of the mysteries of our loving Father. Remember, He is not keeping things from you; He is keeping things *for* you. It is the journey of discovery our Father's love for us (through Jesus and the Holy Spirit) that we live a life of Joy Restored.

Thank Him ahead of time. Thank Him for what you have. He is willing to heal you. He wants to heal you. Say out loud, "Lord, heal my heart, restore my soul, and make me whole. Amen."

Questions to contemplate as you restore your joy:

~ ~ ~ ~ ~

Are you willing to believe healing is available for you?

Do you understand better the difference between guilt and shame?

Are you willing to discover how God has given you a new identity in Christ?

~ ~ ~ ~ ~

Chapter 8

Making Meaning of Your Pain

We are meaning makers. As human beings, we require meaning. Discovering meaning is something we naturally do. We struggle the most when we are unable to understand or make meaning of a situation. This is why CSA is so hideous; as a child, we don't even know or understand the meaning of sex. Then, add *it's a secret* to it, and it sets us up to attach the wrong meaning to it. This chapter will help us get the right meaning attached to it.

We can't control what happened to us in childhood, right? True, but we can control the meaning we attach to it, especially as adults. Our ability and willingness to go through this process is what moves us from victim to victor.

Here's the thing about giving meaning to your current situation: you have already given meaning to your situation based on what you learned growing up. But is it accurate, right, true? Once again, we need to look at what we have learned so we can unlearn it, override it, get a new updated version. We get to voluntarily move into the process of becoming fully human. This process isn't easy, and most people don't ever do it, even those who haven't been sexually abused. Giving up the meanings you have attached to yourself and your past can feel like dying. Parts of yourself have become frozen because of the abuse, and you need to have conversations with those parts of you and bring words to it. When you do, you can release the wrong meanings and identities and let them die. You can't make an empowering meaning of the pain until you recognize the disempowering meaning you have given it.

Making meaning of our pain involves our thinking and our imagination, including curiosity and wonder. Curiosity and wonder release liberating energies that help you grow and heal. Curiosity is having an active interest, a genuine desire to know more about something. It creates an openness to unfamiliar experiences, laying the groundwork for greater opportunities to experience discovery, joy, and delight. It is essentially a search for discovery of meaning in life.

Being a God girl, I believe that meaning comes from our Daddy in Heaven. This is not our home. We are temporarily on this planet in these physical earth suits to learn about our real home in the spiritual realm. We are here in the natural to learn about the supernatural. The unseen is more powerful than the seen. This is a journey of being...being human so our spirit can become more like our Daddy's. We are created in His image, and this experience here in the physical helps us mature into His image. He created us to have a relationship with Him. It's amazing to me to think that He wants a relationship with us. That He wants to know us. That He wants to comfort us. That He wants to help us. That He has a good plan for us.

This is a journey of being.

In our humanness, we have a difficult time believing He has a good plan for us when we have been very hurt. It is the age-old question of *why does God let bad things happen?* The age-old answer is that we have free will. The Creator of the universe didn't want a bunch of preprogrammed robots. He wanted human beings who could choose to love Him or not. Who could choose good or evil. Who could choose to be selfish or selfless. Who could choose to put their desires above hurting other people, like sexually abusing a child.

We get to choose what we believe. I remember battling with this whole thing about free will, thinking I would have made a world of robots who loved me automatically. Then, wrong choices of the robots hurting each other couldn't even be made. But I'm not God and neither are you.

I have learned that overcoming evil and growing through the evil that has happened to me has made me a better human. I am less judgmental, more kind, more compassionate. For example, when my narcissistic wasband (ex-husband) discarded and replaced me (my story of overcoming is for another book), I got a new compassion for divorced women. Before that happened to me, I use to think divorce was always the woman's fault. She couldn't please her husband, she was a nag, or whatever. I was so judgmental about it, I even had a crude statement I would say. Oh, how wrong I was. Finding myself in that position, there was nothing I could have done. When he found his replacement, I was dumped. It wasn't my fault.

From that moment on, I changed my view of divorced women. I related to them on a whole different level. It got me thinking about how I feel when I meet other people who have overcome similar situations. I recognize the instant bond between us. Going through similar situations brings us closer to others, and it doesn't necessarily have to be a bad situation either. It can be something simple like having gone to Disneyland. You instantly have something you can relate to with each other.

Back to the age-old question and free will. All experiences, good or bad, help us relate to one another. We have been given the ability to choose how these experiences will impact us in the future. We can be bitter or better. We can choose to believe these experiences help us to become more Christ-like, less selfish. I truly hope you hear my love for you in these words. I am not downplaying what has happened to you. What happened was horrible. I am saying (with love) that in order to have a healed heart, you get to make a choice. You can remain a victim or move into victory. You are not that child anymore. Yes, what happened impacted you negatively, but now as an adult, you can let go of the pain of it and choose to heal. Choose to believe God has a plan for you, that He can bring good from evil (Romans 8:28). Believe that having free will lets you be transformed into His image by the renewing of your mind (Romans 8:12).

Let go of the pain of it and choose to heal.

Let's work on renewing your mind so you can reclaim your identity in Christ! Let's work on making meaning from your pain. Let's take your mess and make it a message.

Questions to contemplate as you restore your joy:

~ ~ ~ ~ ~

Can you become curious and begin exploring making meaning of your pain?

Do you see how your experiences could help someone else?

Can you shine light into the darkness?

~ ~ ~ ~ ~

Chapter 9

Change Your Surroundings

Most of this book so far has been intangible. It has been more about your thinking – how the abuse affected your thinking and how you are in control and able to change your thinking. By choosing to believe you have this ability to change your thoughts, it begins to bring change in your life. By choosing to believe that our Heavenly Father gave you this ability begins to change things. The very energy, vibrations, you create by choosing to believe brings change. You were created in the image of the Creator of the universe. We are co-creators with Him. You are not powerless. You get to choose to believe or not. When you choose to believe in Jesus Christ, you have the power of the Holy Spirit in you. Then, you do not have to depend on your will power to have joy restored in your life; it is by the power of the Holy Spirit in you.

You get to learn about your Creator and the power He has given you, and you will be fully restored. You will have double for your trouble and everlasting joy will be yours (Isaiah 61:7). He is the God of restoration – that means in addition to repaying you for every wrong done, but He'll go above and beyond to make things even better than they would have been had you never been abused.

See what I mean by all of this being intangible so far? It's all in the unseen realm, and if I haven't said it before I will say it now...the unseen is more powerful than the seen. The seen does have power though, and that is what this chapter is about.

> ***The unseen is more powerful than the seen.***

Your surroundings have an impact on you. How you keep your home and your car will affect your attitude, and your attitude affects your thinking, and your thinking affects your actions. We have talked a lot about your thinking, and now let's look at some actions you can take, because the above cycle can be reversed. Your actions affect your thinking, and your thinking affects your attitude, so to have a better attitude, you can change your actions.

Let's start with this example: making your bed. (If you already make your bed, think of a different habit you would like to do but aren't doing.) To me, I felt like *why make the bed when I will just be messing it up again and no one will see it but me?* Notice my rationale? We all rationalize our actions. We all have motives for what we do or don't do. There's something deeper that drives us to action or inaction. All this healing – renewing, reclaiming, restoring – is about uncovering what drives us and the thought process behind it.

As I was on this journey for myself, I started recognizing how not making my bed in the morning (because no one else would see it but me) was giving myself the message that I wasn't worth it. I wasn't worth having a clean environment. I wasn't worth the energy. That awareness brought more awareness, which is the awesome thing about healing: You begin to spiral upward instead of downward. I became aware that when I walked into the room, I could feel better about myself if the bed was made. That is when I decided to take the simple action and see if that would be true.

I made my bed the next morning, and sure enough, when I walked into my bedroom later in the day and saw that made bed, I felt good about myself. It was a little step and had such a powerful impact on me. There are actions you can take in your life that will seem so little yet make a huge difference. Every small step makes the journey move forward.

My next opportunity to take action to change feelings I had about myself was in the kitchen. I had pretty much the same rationale about the kitchen as I did about making my bed. It was just going to get messy again, and no one was going to see it but me, right? I had started listening to Joyce Meyer's teachings, and one day she said something like this: "If you can't take control over your dirty dishes, how do you expect to take control over anything else?"

At that point in my life, I would let the dishes pile up in the sink and on the counter until I needed them washed...and that was only when I had nothing clean left to use. Old food would be crusted on, and dishes left to soak in the sink would stink. Not a pretty sight. I started realizing it was more work to clean them after having let them sit than to stay on top of it. I also recognized how horrible seeing the mess made me feel, and those feelings led to thoughts about being a horrible person.

Spiraling down was no longer an option for me. I was so tired of being a victim and *poor me* that I started taking different action. I created a little system. After using any kind of kitchen utensil, I would rinse it and put it upside down in the sink. No water to pool and get stinky and no more dried on stuff. It was the least I could do, a small step, but set the journey to keeping a clean kitchen. Yes, sometimes the sink would be so full of rinsed-off dishes that I would have to unload the dishwasher in order to load it again, but it was super quick. No more scrubbing – just a fast unload and reload.

Another powerful thing you can do is get rid of clutter. Things you haven't used for a year can be sold or given away. As you create a more clean, orderly space in your life, you are creating space to grow spiritually. Keep your countertops clean. Make your bed. Change the pictures on your walls. Paint your walls. What you see affects you. You are worthy of a clean environment. You are worthy to create an environment for yourself that you will enjoy. You are showing yourself that you are valuable by taking the time and energy to change your surroundings. You are valuable! You are a daughter of a King!

Questions to contemplate as you restore your joy:

~ ~ ~ ~ ~

Do you make your bed and keep your kitchen clean?

What small steps can you take to change your surroundings to create a space that shows you value yourself?

What does the inside of your car look like?

~ ~ ~ ~ ~

Third Key:

Restore Your Joy

Chapter 10

Everything is Energy

You can Google this chapter's title and find tons of scientific evidence to support this fact: Everything is energy. Quantum physics provides the evidence. God is the One who created energy. We humans cannot create or destroy energy, but we can transform it. For example, eating. A sandwich has energy (calories for our bodies to burn and absorb), and when we eat it, its energy transforms into an energy that feeds our bodies. You can also think of energy as vibrations. Basically, that's what energy is: movement, vibration, frequency.

Common forms of energy include either solid mass or non-solid matter, such as heat, light, electrical, sound, gravitational, potential (stored energy), and kinetic (energy of motion). We don't create these things; we discover what God has already put into place. We come to understand and use what the Creator of the universe designed for us to use. There's so much to know in life about how God designed everything, and my goal with this book and the Innocent Again program is to give you the pieces of knowledge you need to move from victim to victor. You already have the ability to do this. Now let's get to applying it.

Let's talk some more about accepting yourself and being gracious to yourself right now with where you are at in life. The choices you have made as an adult have gotten you to where you are. You made the best choices at the time based on what you knew, your attitude, and your beliefs. You have done the best you could with the information and experiences you had. As a CSA survivor, speaking for myself, so many of the choices I made were not in my best interest, even when I thought they were.

Accepting yourself is the best energy you can create to speed up your ability to experience joy. You get to choose how you feel about yourself. You get to choose if you will believe that God loves you and created you and sent His Son to die for you so you can be set free from your past and have a clean slate. You get to make that choice every day, every hour, every minute.

You get to choose how you feel about yourself.

When you choose to feel bad about yourself, beat yourself up, remain in a pity party, you use the same energy; the very energy you could have used to make a better choice for yourself. Don't waste it on beating yourself up. Put down the club, it only keeps you stuck. Use that energy to accept yourself and build yourself up, not tear yourself down. Choose to use your energy for what makes you feel good. Accept where you are now. Use your energy wisely.

Accepting yourself is also forgiving yourself. Unforgiveness is a huge energy drain. Like beating yourself up uses the energy you need to heal, unforgiveness also uses the energy you need to heal and have a joy-restored life. There are many misconceptions about forgiveness. The main thing forgiveness does is disconnects the connection between you and the person you need to forgive. Forgiveness is something you do for yourself, not for them. As a matter of fact, you don't even have to tell them you forgave them. I forgave my wasband for alienating me from my children, and I have never told him that. I forgave him so that I could stop feeling sorry for myself. Remember, feeling sorry for yourself takes energy, the energy you need to heal – the energy I needed to heal.

Everything is energy. Every emotion has energy. There are positive and negative energies around every emotion, thought, and word. Use your energy wisely. Not only is unforgiveness a huge energy drain, it also keeps you stuck in the past. Its very nature is about something that happened in your past, which you have no ability to change. It's impossible to change the past. What happened, happened. It was horrible. It was tragic. It changed the trajectory of your life, and now you can intentionally change the trajectory from victim to victor. Forgiving is part of that process.

Forgiveness has layers, especially with CSA, because the wound is so emotionally and physiologically hurtful. You **can** heal from it though. It won't necessarily be easy, but it is doable. God has given you the ability to do it. You can choose to believe that. Believing is a positive energy and can help you to forgive for your sake.

Forgiveness might be really difficult for you like it was for me when I got hurt as an adult to forgive my narc wasband for discarding me. My first step was to pray for the ability to even want to forgive. I had no desire, whatsoever, to forgive him. Even though I knew forgiving him wasn't for him, it was for me, I still didn't want to. It felt like I was betraying myself if I forgave him. I was so devastated and so hurt, and basically wanted to feel sorry for myself. I was being a victim just like I had when I didn't forgive my dad for sexually abusing me. I was staying stuck and being miserable. Little by little, I started remembering things I had learned, the things I am teaching you, and started climbing out of the pit. Start where you are with forgiveness. We are all in different places of healing and walking with our Daddy.

This leads to another huge energy drain: comparison. There is no win in comparison. Comparing gets you nowhere. You either feel better than someone or worse than someone, and neither of those feelings create empowering energies. Comparing is one of the main ingredients in how to stay in a pity party and remain a victim. Abuse is abuse, pain is pain, and what is traumatic for one person may not be as traumatic or painful for another person. Sexual abuse interferes with being the person you were made to be. It's a set up to believe lies of the devil, to believe lies about yourself, lies like *there is something wrong with me, I am broken, I am to blame, it's my fault, I'll never be loved.* To compare your abuse to someone else's is a no-win situation. Either you feel like yours was so much worse and there's no hope for you, or that yours wasn't bad enough so you shouldn't even complain about it.

I have seen this more than once in women I have interviewed: The less traumatic the abuse, the more psychological the damage. It's almost like because their abuse wasn't blatant enough, they don't think they need any kind of healing. They minimize their pain by comparing and never end up with the peace and joy Jesus died for them to have. I have seen this in my own extended family with two sisters. One got sexually abused by their dad and the other one didn't. The one who didn't ended up more miserable in her adult life, becoming morbidly obese, sitting in front of a mirror that only showed her face, applying and reapplying makeup for hours, and never went out of the house because she believed the lie that something was wrong with her since her dad hadn't chosen her.

Comparison is a negative energy. We want to be using our energy wisely.

Questions to contemplate as you restore your joy:

~ ~ ~ ~ ~

Is the concept of everything being energy new to you?

Do you see how certain feelings have draining energy?

Do you see how certain feelings have empowering energy?

~ ~ ~ ~ ~

Chapter 11

The Power of Responsibility

Responsibility...what a complex word when it comes to CSA. The way our brains work, wanting us to feel a sense of control in out-of-control situations, especially as children without fully developed brains, we will take on responsibility for things that are not our responsibility. Our brains always try to create a feeling of safety. By giving us the thought that we are responsible, then we think we have a level of control, and thereby tries to satisfy the safety need. Our brain always wants us to feel safe, but as children, we weren't safe, we weren't responsible, and we weren't in control. If our brain had allowed us to feel how unsafe we were, we would have had a mental breakdown. We would have curled up in a little ball and willed ourselves dead. And some of you may have done that.

But you didn't die. You went on living, and to go on living, your brain tried to help you by making you feel responsible like something was wrong with you. You somehow made it happen, and you can somehow make it stop. Now, as an adult, you can use your brain to recognize that it wasn't true. You were not responsible, and you could not have prevented it from happening. As an adult, you may be hanging onto the feeling of being responsible because you don't want to feel the pain of how you were hurt. The way to release this feeling of responsibility is to let yourself feel the feelings of not being responsible as a child.

Responsibility is your ability to respond.

See yourself as the helpless victim you were. Let yourself cry for that little, innocent child. Let yourself grieve for what was stolen from that innocent child. Be careful not to shortcut the grieving process, or you could short-circuit the healing process. Feelings buried alive never die, and those helpless feelings that you didn't let yourself feel as a child are safe to come out now. That is how we move from unhealthy responsibility to healthy responsibility.

Here is a healthy way to look at responsibility: It is our ability to respond. As children, we didn't have the ability to respond correctly. We couldn't even understand the magnitude of what was happening to us, let alone respond in our best interest. We were told to keep it a secret. That this was a special relationship. That we were being loved. That it was in our best interest, all the while being groomed in a multitude of ways to be used by our predator.

This was so difficult for me to grasp. Because of the decisions I made as a teenager and young adult, I totally felt responsible. It took counseling to get me to believe otherwise. What I learned was that our decision-making process is damaged by abuse. The decisions that we make before we have processed through not being responsible as a child, teenager, young adult, or even as an adult, are not from a place of truly deciding what would be the best course of action for ourselves. Before processing that we aren't responsible, we only know how to make decisions from a damaged place. We don't know what we don't know yet, and we can't make a good decision without having more information, without an understanding of how our decision making was impacted by the abuse.

This is why I am so happy you are reading this. You are looking to get new, better information. You want to learn how you can take responsibility for your healing now as an adult. You can respond, feel the feelings, and heal. The good news is, you can repair your decision-maker and God will help you do it.

There is powerful, positive energy in taking responsibility. Taking responsibility does not mean you are responsible for what happened; it means you are taking responsibility for how you will respond to what happened. Let's say someone, out of anger, threw a glass pitcher at you, and it hit the floor and shattered. They leave the room. They aren't coming back to clean it up. The broken glass is laying there scattered across the floor. Here's where you have the positive power of responsibility: You get to choose. You can remain trapped by that glass and constantly must move around it, try to not step on it and be continually reminded of it *or* you can clean it up.

You didn't make the mess, but it's affecting you now. If you don't take responsibility and pick up the glass, you are still trapped by it. Walking around it, you are affected by it. The person who threw it doesn't care. It's not their house. They didn't violate their space; they violated your space. It's your responsibility to clean it up. Who cares what they are doing? You care about your life, so you are cleaning up the broken glass. It may not be easy to get all the broken pieces picked up, and after you think you have it all picked up, you may even find a stray piece that slid under the table. You pick it up and get on with your life, not as a victim, but as a victor.

It gets easier to process through the broken pieces as you develop your responsibility muscle. It becomes stronger with use like any muscle does, and as you find those stray pieces of broken glass, you can easily get rid of them. It's your increased ability to respond (responsibility) and clean up a mess you didn't make that will fill your life with joy. You can have joy restored in your life. You are not doing this by yourself. You have this community and most importantly you have the power of the Holy Spirit inside you as a Christian.

I do need to add one very important ingredient to taking responsibility. This ingredient will determine how fast you get those pieces of glass picked up. Remember, everything is energy, and if you are complaining while picking up the pieces, you are negating the positive energy from taking responsibility. You can't get where you want to go by complaining about where you are. Complaining is a subconscious way of expressing that you are powerless to change your circumstances.

Complaining is draining. It zaps your energy, makes you feel hopeless, lowers your self-esteem, and brings the entire atmosphere around you down.

Like Joyce Meyer says, "Complain and remain."

If you do not want to stay where you are, then use your ability to respond and not complain, then watch your life become joy filled!

Questions to contemplate as you restore your joy:

~ ~ ~ ~ ~

How has your thinking about responsibility changed from reading this chapter?

Do you recognize how you are responsible for your healing?

Do you see how complaining can keep you stuck?

~ ~ ~ ~ ~

Chapter 12

Taking Action

Let's put everything together now and live the abundant, joy-filled life Jesus died to give us. You have learned a lot in this little book, and sorry to say that learning alone will not be the thing that makes anything change. Of course, learning and replacing the wrong things we have learned in the past is a huge part of the equation. It's the first step, because you don't know what you don't know, but acting on what you have learned is what makes change. Most of us don't like change, and that's why most people will not live joy-filled lives. They won't do the things that make the change because what change will bring is unknown. Sometimes familiarity, even if it's miserable, seems more comfortable than the unknown. That is why so many people stay in abusive situations. I pray you will have the courage to change. The change from victim to victor is so worth it.

I recommend you start with baby-step actions. Here's a simple one. Take time throughout the day to remember God loves you. Set an alarm on your phone. I have mine set for 9 am, noon, and 5 pm. The alarm is called *God loves me,* and when it goes off, that's what I see on my phone screen. When it goes off and I am with someone, I will tell them it's my God loves me alarm. I have had some sweet encounters with that happening. One time, I was making a purchase and the alarm went off. I told the cashier it was my *God loves me* alarm. She said, "That is so great. I am going to set one up on my mom's phone. She is in the hospital, and it will be so encouraging for her." This is a simple plan of action you can take, and who knows who you else you might help.

As you grow in knowing and feeling secure in God's love for you, taking the right action becomes easier. Love is the greatest motivator. Your action step is to set an alarm at three different times a day to remind yourself God loves you.

Because of CSA, I know it can be difficult to accept that God loves you. I personally know the questions and hurts you have experienced. All I am asking of you is to imagine if it were true. Imagine a good, good God. A Daddy who has the best in store for you. A good future. A Daddy who can bring good out of the bad. One who can give you a peace and a joy that's beyond understanding. Imagine there is something greater than this world we live in. That we are orphans here and have been adopted by the best Dad ever. While we are waiting here for the adoption to be completed, in the meantime we can live in joyful anticipation, trusting the best is yet to come.

When you start to fear or worry, say out loud, "I trust God." Say it over and over till the fear or worry fade away. Trusting is your action step. Renew your mind, reclaim your identity, restore your joy.

> ***You can think thoughts on purpose!***

Action follows acceptance, so acceptance is your next step. Acceptance is understanding what you cannot change. You don't have to like it, condone it, or agree with it, but you must accept the situation for what it is. Accepting is not giving up. Accepting is your starting point. Acceptance puts you in a frame of mind to move forward empowered. It's releasing the past. Also, accept that this world is not your home. That the unseen is more powerful than the seen. That you have the power in you to act and co-create with our Daddy. That is the way He made you. He desires a relationship with you. As you accept this truth, you will act. Accepting is your action step. Renew your mind, reclaim your identity, restore your joy.

Use your God loves me alarm to also notice what you have been thinking about. Check out what kind of energy you surround yourself with. What's going on around you? What are you seeing? What are you hearing? Take action to recognize that you have the ability to control your thoughts. You do not have to think about whatever pops into your head. You can become aware of your energy levels and think thoughts that empower you. You can think thoughts on purpose. Take the time to think about what you want to think on purpose.

Create some affirmations to say when you recognize your thinking has been off. Prepare yourself for battle. The battle is in the mind, and you choose your thoughts. Bring yourself into the moment and realize right now in this moment, I have all that I need. I am okay. I am loved. I can do all things through Christ who gives me strength. I am not alone. Every day in every way I am getting stronger and stronger. Peace and joy surround me, they are mine for the taking. I choose joy. I choose peace. Your action step is to change your negative thought to a positive thought. Renew your mind, reclaim your identity, restore your joy.

Watch the words you are speaking about yourself.

Here's another great action step to take and it's so simple! Whenever you say something negative about yourself (like if I eat one potato chip, I have to eat the whole bag), add these three, life-changing, empowering words at the end: *up until now*. Using the above example, if I eat one potato chip, I have to eat the whole bag *up until now*. Whatever negative thing you say, add those three words at the end. I can't keep my kitchen clean *up until now*. I can't forgive my dad *up until now*. Those three words change the energy around what you just spoke and give you power. They will change your life!

Your action step is to become aware of your words so that you can negate the negative with *up until now*. You have the God-given power to do this. Renew your mind, reclaim your identity, restore your joy.

Here are the five action steps in one word per step: Love, Trust, Accept, Think, and Speak. You can do all these things with the power of the Holy Spirit in you. You can do the three R's: renew your mind, reclaim your identity, restore your joy. Our Daddy wants you to have the abundant life. It's yours for the taking.

Questions to contemplate as you restore your joy:

~ ~ ~ ~ ~

What is the hardest step for you?

Is there any step you feel like you have already taken?

Can you imagine a healed you?

~ ~ ~ ~ ~

The Best is Yet to Come!

It has been such an honor to share with you what has helped me and other ladies to have joy restored. I pray this has helped you along your journey to *Innocent Again*. If you have a personal relationship with Jesus Christ, you are already *Innocent Again*. He has wiped the slate clean. He has given you access to Father God. He is the way, the truth, and the life. Jesus died so we can be *Innocent Again,* free from sin, shame, and guilt. There is now no more condemnation for those who are in Christ Jesus. Oh, how freeing that is! All you need to do is walk in that truth by renewing your mind and reclaiming your identity in Christ, and your joy will be restored.

Have you ever given your life to Jesus? Would you like to?

If you are ready to commit your life to Jesus and follow Him, all you have to do is ask Him to forgive your sins. He gives you a fresh start to live the life He had designed for you all along. Begin by praying this prayer...

Lord Jesus, thank You for giving Your life for me and forgiving me of my sins so I can have a personal relationship with You. I am sincerely sorry for the mistakes I have made and release the lies I have believed; lies that have kept me from living the abundant, joy-filled life You gave Your life for me to have. I need You to help me live right.

Your Word says in Romans 10:9, "If you declare with your mouth, 'Jesus is Lord,' and believe in your heart that God raised Him from the dead, you will be saved" (NIV). I believe You are the Son of God and confess You as my Savior and Lord. Take me just as I am, and work in my heart, making me the person You want me to be. I want to live for You, Jesus, and I am so grateful You are giving me a fresh start in my new life with You today. I love You, Jesus! Amen!

If you prayed this prayer for the first time or recommitted to walking with Jesus, email us at support@innocentagain.com. We would like to help you with free, online resources to help you make progress in pursuing everything God has for you.

The best is yet to come!

About the Author

Jeanette Finn is the founder and president of Innocent Again, a nonprofit organization that is restoring joy into the lives of victims of childhood sexual abuse. Jeanette is a survivor of emotional and sexual abuse by her father and wasband. She has been set free from nicotine, marijuana, alcohol, gluttony, pornography, and poverty. Jeanette's personal experience of overcoming and finding joy has created a deep desire to help others to overcome their past and their addictions. Through a powerful process she had her joy restored and now helps others overcome their own painful experiences and distorted thinking. Her purpose and passion is to set wounded souls free to be Innocent Again.

Jeanette is happily remarried to her husband Mike and lives in the Pacific Northwest where they enjoy the plentiful hiking and biking the area provides. They love traveling to sun-soaked beaches during the winter months.

Renew, Reclaim, Restore! No more secrets! Remember, we can become #innocentagain and help others do the same!

Visit www.InnocentAgain.com to learn more about how to get support or donate.

CPSIA information can be obtained
at www.ICGtesting.com
Printed in the USA
BVHW050211100722
641697BV00001B/95